To Ellen Gammon!
who visited Robben Island
on 07/03/2005

My Freedom,

My Passion

I used Robben Island
to grow and develop
and not allow it to
destroy me'

By
Modise Phekonyane

MY FREEDOM, MY PASSION

© 2004 - Modise Phekonyane
All rights reserved

Edited, produced and distributed by
CPM Publishers, P.O. Box 51722,
West Beach 7449
South Africa

Printed in South Africa by
Kairos Publishing
Tel: + 27 31 4099516
Email: mwkairos@mweb.co.za

MEN OF FREEDOM

Men of freedom
Always have passion
To see a society as a rainbow
A people and not peoples

Men of freedom
Know there's no freedom
While others are superior
And others despised

Men of freedom
Standing on a foundation
And on principles
Guiding principles of freedom

Men of freedom
Gave birth from the belly of Africa
Very young and fragile
Vulnerable but so pretty

Men of freedom
Gave us the rainbow character
That defines who we are
As a rainbow nation

Men of freedom
It's not about wealth
It's not about material
But about who not what we are

Men of freedom
Taught us love conquers all
Prosperity will naturally come
When we own our identity

Men of freedom
Make us glad
To uphold the spirit
Of freedom and unity

Men and women of freedom
Long live!
Long live for your sacrifice
Viva! Viva men of freedom

NOT TEARS OF SUFFERING

Tears of a man
No tears without real pain
Not tears of guilt
Tears of suffering

Running down cheeks
Coming down their faces
Biting their teeth
Faces twitching

Dogs set on them
Removed from the dyke
Exposed to storms
Of North West winds

Storms that blow ships into wrecks
Storms blowing 15 meters high
At extremely high speed
And at time toiling in the rain

Still taught each other
Developed each other
Displayed the very best of Ubuntu
Came out victors and heroes

Long live their soul
Long live their families
Long live South Africa
Long Live!

SCAVENGING

Kept in the land
The land of plenty
But forced to scavenge
Kept ignorant and illiterate

Lived like a slave
Sucked poverty from my mom
Raised only with sense of hope
That things will change

Brought up from the ghettos
By my dad and my father
Poor but courageous
Strong hearted but gentle

Mom and dad together
With no sense of dignity
No pride and reason to live
But they pressed on for us

To put bread on the table
Could not think of beating
The hand that fed them
Even brought us leftovers

In my home I ate
From the masters table
Drowning in anger daily
Could not take it anymore

POISED TO SHOOT

Thirsty and glaring
Roaming the streets
In Hippos and vans
Preying on their prey

Searching for an opportunity
Poised to shoot
Maybe to arrest and incarcerate
For a night or years

Doors slammed and locked
Only to open later
For the master to appear
To flex his muscle on me

Defenseless and vulnerable
Whipping and whipping my skin
The baton cutting my flesh
Open and gashing blood

My skinny body turned blue
Strong arm raised and down
A punch on my ribs
A kick in my behind

Teeth gnashing and lips tight
My neck thick and swollen
From holding back
A cry of pain

NO NIGHT

No night No night No night
Could not stop nor deter
My quest for knowledge
Education and knowledge irreplaceable

No night No night No night
To keep my eyes closed
Not even my heart from beating
Pondering yearning and burning

No night No night No night
Dark enough to stop
My soul to rise
Above the cloud of darkness

No night No night No night
Could suppress my determination
To burst the flood of traps
To be free from my complex

No night No night No night
Of poverty and gloom
Could deter my world
Of freedom to dream

No night No night No night
To shade my focus
From the day of knowledge
Shining in my heart for ever

HELD AND BOUND

Looking and seeing life
Through the key-hole
Of my home temporary
Feeling held and bound
In fear and uncertainty

Tormented emotionally
Day followed by night
Minutes by minutes long
Long until hours like years
Unsure of what time it was

Interrogated vigorously
No mercy shown upon
By captors showing cruelty
Written over their faces
Flowing from their hearts

Pouring and pouring on
Over my tiny body
Like perfume of pain
Battling to understand
The minds of these big men

Shouting and screaming at me
Questions followed by punches
Bad smell of cigarettes and liquor
Under my nose
Scarred and terrified

Shaking and shivering
Tormented wounded and bleeding
Battling to keep my sanity
Hanging on to survive
Never even thinking to give up

THIS KIND OF MAN

Who is that man?
Standing and towering
Over my sleepless body

How can I live?
Without fear
Of his huge presence

Occupying every space
Leaning and learning
To every breath I take

Pondering on the shores
Of my heart
Shaking pillars of my nerves

Suddenly I wonder
Does he have heart
What does he feel

When my dad is not here
Where are his siblings
Would they care

Would they want to know
He is a torturer and abuser
Violator of human rights

THE SECOND TIME AROUND

I have been on this Island
The second time around
For three weeks now
And at the distance
Tried to deal with my past

However I tried to avoid facing it
Who was I fooling
Every time I went past
Even when I meant not to look
Some magnetic memory force

Dragged my attention
Always find myself looking
That would leave my heart swollen
With aching memories of the Island
Was my home once

My heart throbbing
Blood flooding fast uncontrollably
Feeling dizzy and faint
Biting my teeth and clenching my fists
My knees shivering with anger

Taking a deep breath
Closing my eyes and suddenly
Good memories emerge
Voices of men who were my family
Encouraging and mentoring

Their visions and presence
Flushing out bad memories
Pulling back the good of the Island
Unity for survival a must
To overcome and triumph

I HAVE KNOWLEDGE

Only if I can have knowledge
I can go beyond the limit
To do the unthinkable
The difference can be impacted
To change many lives

I am original and you are
With only different colours
And only different languages
The mind and soul the same
The heart and blood together

From the soil we come
To the soil we all will go
This is where we are now
No matter how hard we try
We will always belong together

Hold hands together and share knowledge
The one part of knowledge
Of knowing we belong together
Common things to have and share
Is love, only love

Knowledge removes fear
Never fear no more
Knowledge brings light
Shine together as a unit
Of the same universe

RE-UNITED

What a pleasure
To re-unite with
Reminisce and celebrate our past
Painful past

Trying my best to smile
As always when in pain myself
Holding my emotions back
So that they could be at their best

Their courage still moving me
Shaking the very foundation
Of my inner joy
My heart pounding hard

With excitement this time
To realize my dream true
Hugging laughing joyously
In a free country

That we so hard fought for
So much sacrifice made
For the liberation of all in the land
Freedom reality for the future generation

Their skin a bit rough
Hair worn-out and like snow wool
Their voices still sharp
Eyes deep from past to the far future

Maybe lots of questions asked
As on their faces written
Lines and wrinkled faces
Frowned and still wearing smiles

As we re-unite on the Island
They tried hard to be excited
But obvious echoes of the past
Were written over their faces

Most remained frozen
Unmoved and only their eyes could tell
Some holding tears back
Slowly strolling and coming to terms

After a while then settled
They gave account of their story
Flowing from heart to heart
Still trying to have questions answered

These men I love
These men I respect
These men I know
These men I understand

AM I NORMAL

Someone tried to isolate me
From the main society
The so-called normal society
What is normal in up normal
Can divided people be normal

Only time can bring all together
Together as a people
As a people loyal to the nationhood
And together stuck by common virtues
Loyalty to each other they owe

Beyond ethnicity race and gender
They are glued together
To raise and build a nation
Of champions and victors
Unshaken unmoved from their resolve

COMRADES MENTORS

These are the cornerstones
Of freedom from and to time
As between the walls of prison
My life chiseled by comrades
Character molded and shaped
Confused whether to stay longer
Or to go out quicker

To share my precious experience
Hard way gained and obtained
To influence youth and the rest
In the direction of time essence
Generously given unselfishly
Releasing the potential to growth
Exploring the best from within

But aaah! how painful it is
Now to see time wasted
The abilities and talents squandered
Misuse of able bodies and minds
Time sleeping fast through fingers
Who do we blame
We have no excuse

PLEASED TO ESCAPE

Reality is inescapable
To escape it is a fallacy
But for a moment
I am pleased to escape
To the world so real
Call it a fantasy
But you can call it reality

Freedom my reality
I dreamed freedom always
I have been there so many times
Never wanted to come back
The truth is in the heart
For upon the heart you build
A real world of Freedom

A world of freedom and hope
Hope and faith to desire
To make things happen
Encourage to change things
Freedom a myth or dream
My right to dream
Our right to be really free

So unreal and untouched
Freedom can touch all
Inspired by freedom
Dreaming for a good society
To visualize my freedom
To hire victories life

WOUNDED

Wounded but strong
Wounded in my spirit
And in my heart

Wounded physically
Wounded emotionally
Courageous to live

Wounded and unwanted
Wounded and abandoned
Forsaken and isolated

Wounded and I love
Wounded and cherish all
I love life and love all people

Wounded by love
Wounded and you love
You love me and I love you

DETERMINED TO SHINE

I am determined
Bite my teeth
Pulled myself up
Paddled on through

Aching with desire
To make it
Alas onlookers
Who wish and desire

Desire my breakdown
Wounded against odds
Against the wall
Anxious and eager

Yes I deserve to succeed
I will make it
I will pull through
No matter what

TIME SOONER OR LATER

What is this thing about time
Time yesterday
Time today
Time tomorrow

They always worry about time
Time in the morning
To catch this or that
Time to have this or that

The people rest when there's time
Time to rest
Time to really sleep
Time to wake up

There is time past
There is time coming
Sooner or later
There is always time

Time to laugh
Time to cry and mourn
I love time
It is healing

I was taken away
From home in the morning
Very early in the morning
That was the beginning of time

Time went out - passed
Days came and went
Weeks came and went
Years went by and I got home in time

I never knew love
I never got to care
I lost touch with time
After all, that was the idea

To confuse me with time
Time is very important
Yes absolutely no matter how little

BACKWARD NEVER

Let's make use of time
While we really can
There is only one way for time
To go forward only

Backward never
To uphold the future
Time is good and tough
Time make friends and enemies

It is torturous on memories
It makes the heart ponder
Time for reconciliation the best way
Maybe to deal with time itself

Time taught and developed
Lessons learnt over time
There was only one way
To learn and time to absorb

Seek no passed time
But be drawn in knowledge
How much and how far
Only time will dictate

To me time is measured
Not by the hour nor minute
But by how much and long can I
Rise, walk and search

For knowledge to know
Am fearful to loose out on time
But determined not to give up
On myself and others in time

If it's not on your side
Make time
Or time will make you
Lest you loose it completely

We were not always blessed with time
By the government and the guards
Who sought to destroy us
Mentally and emotionally

To render inmates useless
Using time to deny us opportunities
However, no regrets
For the time spent

On the Island of knowledge
Deeper in spirit and wisdom
Here and now time to move on
To succeed against all odds in time

VOICES UNHEARD

Songs unsung
Voices unheard
Visions unseen
Potential yet untapped

Hoping and hoping
Willing and determined
Unchained and unchanged
Gutsy and courageous

Tomorrow that never was
Yesterday that never will be
Dreams undiscovered
Backward never

EVEN DOGS WERE SHOCKED

Had not seen the rise of sun
That day of my arrest
Denied the pleasure
To rise from relative comfort
Of my family house

Built from second hand material
Sleeping interrupted by knocks
Followed by kicking the door
By the brutal less caring police
Suddenly all woken up, me and all

Peace and tranquility of night
Disturbed by their presence
Even dogs were shocked
Out of their nightly wanderings
As they swung guns freely

Torches all over the house
Flashing in our faces
Me the only one still in bed
Enormous torch lights blinding
Shout and enquiring noise woke me up

Who are you
What's your identity
They knew who I was
A finger pointing me out
Couldn't see due to light

The face hidings behind torches
That finger denied me
The right to see and experience
The rise of the sun
The beautiful sun on Africa

ROBBEN ISLAND MY HOME

Oh Robben Island
My home and refuge
For a while kept me
For a moment preserved me

I faced my life and future
Behind your prison doors
Within the confines of your thick walls
Built by men, my family and mentors

Their blood and sweat
Souls and banished bodies
Shoulders and blistered hands
Open cracked backs

Whipped and sjambokked a million times
Freedom to talk denied
The right to good health not given
Impoverished and to death starved

Trampled upon even by criminals
Policed by criminals
Humiliated by young prison guards
Dogs set, chased and bitten by

Pushed to the maximum
Lowered to treatment of animals
Bleeding from the depth of hearts
Eyes narrowed from sharp stones flying

Of rocks and broken pieces
As they mined the stone
Molding with small hammers
And chisels making brick

From the stone
This very prison today stands
For their incarceration and captivity
For me and my other family too

Many of us from all over
The belly of South Africa
Even a field as Namibia
Settled uncomfortably

In that Robben Island prison
We broke free to share
In our unity for survival
More unity and unity in diversity

As we shared letters
Photographs of sisters and brothers
Mothers and fathers children alike
All left behind

All protected from our pains
Shielded by distance and prison doors
From the suffering we experience
Ill treatment, beating and brutality

The eyes of prisoners
Blinking a lot from keeping tears
Keeping our focus and attention
On the dream and vision

Of our freedom for all
Freedom for us from prison
Free as a nation and a people
Free from hate and segregation

Yes! Yes! Our freedom
The freedom has come
That freedom
That which we fought for

But is it real freedom
When where and how free
Can we say freedom at last
I saw it in our sufferings

I see it in our victory
It may mean different things
To different people
But to real people it is freedom

Those near and very far
Within individuals and without
Indeed we are free
Time is on our side to heal

I LOVE PEOPLE

So hard I tried
Much of the time
Pursuing endlessly
The passion and compassion

For the love of people
Oozing blood
Flooding with compassion
Imbued with energy

Full of hope
For future and tomorrow
For generations today and future
Expectant and eager

I feel tired
Powerless and fatigued
Withdrawn from all
Drained to the bone

But suddenly thoughts
Of my country
And a people
On my feet I rise

I don't give up
Please don't prolong
Embrace and uphold
Courage and determination

My love your love
Our love for life
My heart and blood pledge
I remain unmoved for you

NO ONE LIKE YOU

You are the best
For no one is like you
Unique in all your ways

The best among
Who is questioning
Your strength and beauty

You flow with water
Streams, rivers and dews
Mountains hills and valleys

Gold, diamond and silver
Embedded in your stomach
Unearthed but taken away

Young ladies and men
Of your future so smart
Give them the best

Of your mind
Your soul
And much of your spirit

Why so silent Mother
Why father? Why?
Children fading

You can rise
You can restore
The land to it's best

FOR MY PEOPLE

My many choices
The right to choose
What I wanted to be
Could have any way

I disappointed selfishness
Put down my narrow success
I chose to fight
For my people

My family had expected
Much from me
An intelligent son
Very special in many ways

I let them all down
I gained more than a family
I got more than personal success
Comrades mentors and freedom

I chose to open my heart
To my country and the nation
I chose suffering
So as to earn freedom

I made the best
Of pain and suffering
So I can be a better man
And appreciate freedom

I ceased to exist in self
I sought to be broader
To embrace life at best
Only to be a better man

THE LIGHT SHINES ALWAYS

Can the good come from the bad
Can the worst bring forth the best
If only the good is good
It can prevail above the bad
For it is meant to change

The light always shines
Above darkness it shines
Darkness never conquers light
So is the good over the bad
It brings hope and joy

The best is best
For it has overcome the worst
Time is of the essence
To test the best of the worst
When the best emerges it stays

The good and best people
And the ones to look up to
They have conquered
And are made the best
By the test of time and conditions

Stand men and women
Be of good character
Not for yourselves but the rest
Hopes expectations you carry
For now and years to come
He died not so much
But lived so much
For freedom and dignity
For integrity and harmony

STRIPPED OF ONESELF

Denied to be
Rights taken away
Stripped of oneself
Confused and wandering

Self - denial imposed
A thing of the day
A way of life
Inferior not superior

Bottled and bitter
Turned to hate self
Killing fields inside
Wars of self hate

Made and convinced
I am nothing
But I am someone
I bow for no one

There comes rain
To clean sins
Of oppression and hate
The time is different

The wind has blown
To set me free
I am alive
I love myself

MY EARS STRETCHED

Beyond the walls
My thoughts go beyond
My ears stretched
I hear the voices

I take the command
From beyond the wall
I pass it on to others
The message

Of courage and strength
To march on
To hope on
Beyond walls

Mine was the desire
To inspire others
Beyond the sea
To know my strength

Lies in their hope
For future and tomorrow
Hand in hand beyond
The walls and sea

We march to freedom
Open my heart and read
Beyond seasons and sea
Message of a people free

THE STANDARD SET

Set me free
I demand freedom
His soul cried loud
From inside he demanded

He set the path
He set the pace
He set the standard
For so many to follow

He lived for principles
He pursued principled life
He upheld the principles
Long live!

THE SURVIVAL

We survived
I survived

They survived
All we survived

As determined
To survive

And very strong
Made to survive

As willed
Survived on

To serve
We survive

To overcome
Past for the future

MY QUEENS AND PRINCESSES

They are my mothers
My queens and princesses
The real ladies of character
Strong hearted and kind

They are my ladies
I love them more
Than I can think
They are the best

They stood the test
Of time past brutality
Of pain and suffering
Stripped of dignity

And self respect
Reduced to ashes
Treated like slaves
In the land of birth

Chased and scattered
Silenced and muted
Sentenced to gallows
And exiled even longer

My princesses and queens
Came back to claim
Their position to fight
For freedom united

Never looked back
Forward they went
To wage the struggle
Against segregation

United against corruption
Exploitation and oppression
But still raised the nation
Still fed the nation

Still loved their husbands
Still loved their children
And went on to free us
Long live mothers

I Am The Son

The son of a people
Great people of South Africa
Powerful people
I am the son

I am proud to be yours
I belong here to you
I never know too much
For you are too large

I am only a small piece
That proudly fits in you
The mighty colors
Of my country

The people of South Africa
You make me strong
You are so strong
Never can I ask for more

You gave so much
You still give more
You are so selfless
You embrace the rest

With humility and wisdom
Pride and courage
You're a blessing
For the world abound

You walk tall
With diligence
You are dignified
In spite of a few bad faces

You take strides short
Medium and long
You're blessed with patience
But focused and steadfast

Long live
Long live
Long live
Long live

BELIEVE AND CONTINUE

Don't ask anyone
Blame no one
Despise nor hate none

Have character
Be strong
Have hope

Believe and continue
Uphold the good and beauty
Be positive

Courageous and wise
In all endeavors
Look only ahead and march

Change what you can
Persist in earnest
Ask blame and hate none

TRAPPED IN ISOLATION

Grrr   Grrr   Grrr
Pump Pump Pump
Water coming out
Mixed with the mud and sand

Flushing with tears
Of children back home
Missing their parents
Their uncles and grandpa

The sun blistering hot
Wheelbarrow pulled not pushed
Blisters cracked open
Swollen shoulders

Trapped in isolation
Faces and appearance unknown
Spirit unwilling to die
Hope in the Island of no hope

TIME CLICKING

Time clicking
Every moment clicking
For my life clicking

Not sure what is coming
Not sure what to expect
Every minute frightening

Willing to face death
Determined to stand the pain
Every time the door opened

I was expecting the worst
I had prepared myself
For life on the other side of freedom

Freedom not to think any more
For my part I would have played
For the beautiful people of the land

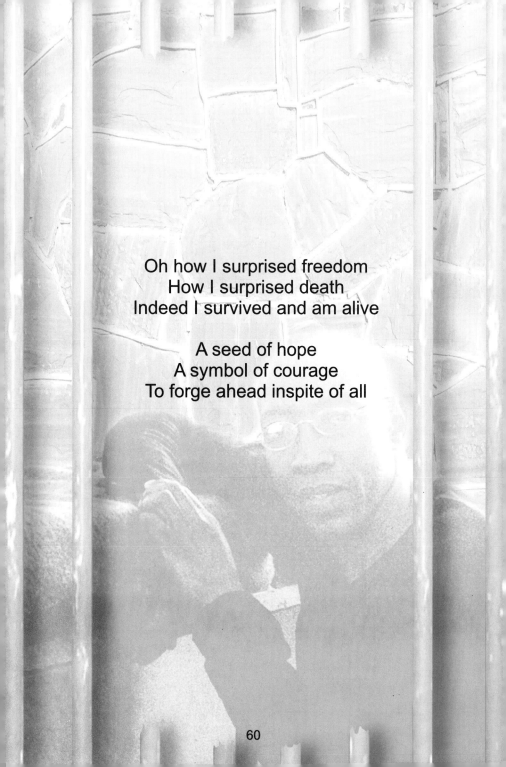

Oh how I surprised freedom
How I surprised death
Indeed I survived and am alive

A seed of hope
A symbol of courage
To forge ahead inspite of all

THE GOAL WITHIN GRASP

Trapped within
Boiling with frustration
Unable to do a thing
Nothing about my surroundings

The goal within grasp
Vision of a free nation
Free from fear and anger
Together marching forward

The picture well clear
Vivid clear in my mind
Of a non racial and equal society
But all bottled up and chained

Unable to manifest physical freedom
Time spent fighting the system
Shot at randomly
Arrested incarcerated and exiled

My passion for freedom
Willing to die for
From beginning to end
For the best of mankind

Notes